RIZAL'S OWN STORY OF HIS LIFE

BERGENLINE
... PRESS ...

Rizal's Own Story of His Life

By José Rizal

José Rizal

Translated by Charles Derbyshire
Editor: Austin Craig

Philippines
1918

CONTENTS

RIZAL.

Sketched by himself in Berlin when he was twenty-five years old. Physicians then told him that he had consumption; but with care, and fresh air, he soon became well again.

RIZAL'S "HYMN TO LABOR"

Words by José Rizal

(Arranged from Chas. Derbyshire's translation; lines in different order.)

Tune of "The Wearing of the Green"

RIZAL'S "MARIA CLARA'S LULLABY"

Words by José Rizal

(Chas. Derbyshire's translation)

Music by Juan Hernandez

THE AUTHOR AT 14

THE MEMORY OF RIZAL

The Memory of Rizal is kept alive in many ways:

1. A province near Manila bears his name.

2. The anniversary of his death is a public holiday.

3. A memorial school has been built by the Insular Government in his native town.

4. His home in exile has been made a national park.

5. The first destroyer of the future Philippine navy is named "Rizal".

6. Rizal's portrait appears on the two-peso bill.

7. Rizal's portrait appears on the two-centavo postage stamp.

MY BOYHOOD

José Rizal wrote the first three chapters in 1878.
He was seventeen years old at that time.

CHAPTER I

MY BIRTH AND EARLIEST YEARS IN KALAMBA

I was born on Wednesday, the nineteenth of June, 1861. It was a few days before the full of the moon. I found myself in a village. I had some slight notions of the morning sun and of my parents. That is as much as I can recall of my baby days.

The training which I received from my earliest infancy is perhaps what formed my habits. I can recall clearly my first gloomy nights, passed on the azotea of our house. They seem as yesterday! They were nights filled with the poetry of sadness and seem near now because at present my days are so sad. On moonlight nights, I took my supper on the azotea. My nurse, who was very fond of me, used to threaten to leave me to a terrible but imaginary being like the bogey of the Europeans if I did not eat.

I had nine sisters and a brother. Our father was a model parent. He gave us the education which was suitable in a family neither rich nor poor. He was thrifty. By careful saving, he was able to build a stone house. He also bought another house; and he put up a nipa cottage on our plot of irrigated ground. The cottage was shaded by bananas and trees.

At nightfall, my mother had us all say our prayers together. Then we would go to the azotea or to a window to enjoy the moonlight; and my nurse would tell us stories. Sometimes sad and sometimes gay, nurse's stories were always oriental in their imagination. In these stories, dead people, gold, and plants on which diamonds grew were all mixed together.

When I was four years of age, my little sister Concha died, and for the first time I cried because of love and sorrow. Till then

I had shed tears only for my own faults, which my loving, prudent mother well knew how to correct.

I learned to write in my own village. My father looked after my education. He paid an old man, who had been his schoolmate, to teach me the first steps in Latin. This teacher lived in our house till he died, five months later. He had been in almost perfect health and it was at the moment of death that he received extreme unction.

Mrs. Rizal-Mercado and her two daughters, Saturnina, the eldest, and Trinidad, then a baby

In June of 1868, I went to Manila with my father. That was just after the birth of Trinidad, the third sister younger than myself. We went in a casco which turned out to be a clumsy boat. I shall not try to tell how happy I was at each new stop on the banks of the Pasig. Beside this same river, a few years later, I was to be very sad. We went to Cainta, Taytay, and Antipolo, and then to Manila. In Santa Ana I visited my eldest sister, Saturnina, who at that time was a student in La Concordia College. Then I returned to my village and remained until 1870.

A dog and cayman combat modeled at Dapitan in 1894. The dog was Rizal's own, and looked like one that had been his boyhood companion at Kalamba

Where Rizal went to school in Biñan: site of Master Justiniano's house, which burned down many years ago

CHAPTER II

My Schooling in Biñan

Biñan is a town about one and one-half hour's drive from my own town, Kalamba. My father was born in Biñan, and he wished me to go there to continue the study of Latin, which I had just begun. He sent me over one Sunday in the care of my brother. The parting from my family was tearful on the side of my parents and my sisters, but I was nine years old and managed to hide my own tears. We reached Biñan at nightfall. We went to an aunt's house where I was to live. When the moon came up, a cousin took me around the town. Biñan appeared to me large and wealthy but neither attractive nor cheerful.

My brother left me after he presented me to the schoolmaster, who, it seemed, had been his own teacher. The schoolmaster was a tall, thin man with a long neck and a sharp nose. His body leaned slightly forward. He wore a shirt of sinamay that had been woven by the deft fingers of Batangas women. He knew Latin and Spanish grammar by heart; but his severity, I believe now, was too great. This is all that I remember of him. His classroom was in his own house, only some thirty meters from my aunt's home.

When I entered the classroom for the first time, he said to me:

"You, do you speak Spanish?"

"A little, sir," I answered.

"Do you know Latin?"

"A little, sir," I again answered.

Because of these answers, the teacher's son, who was the worst boy in the class, began to make fun of me. He was some years my elder and was taller than I, yet we had a tussle. Somehow or other, I don't know how, I got the better of him. I bent him down over the class benches. Then I let him loose, having hurt only his pride. After this, possibly because of my small size, my schoolmates thought me a clever wrestler. On going from the class one boy challenged me. He offered me my hold, but I lost and came near breaking my head on the sidewalk.

I do not want to take up time with telling about the beatings I got, nor shall I attempt to say how it hurt when I received the first ruler blow on my hand. I used to win in the competitions, for no one happened to be better than I. I made the most of these successes. But in spite of the reputation I had of being a good boy, rare were the days in which my teacher did not call me up to receive five or six blows on the hand. When I went out with my companions, they jokingly called me nicknames. But individually they used to be so kind to me that I thought little of their teasings. A few of them were very good and always treated me well. Among these few was a second cousin of mine. Later, some of them were my schoolmates in Manila and then it became my turn to tease.

Near the house of my teacher, Justiniano Aquin Cruz, lived his father-in-law, generally called Juancho. Juancho was an aged artist who let me help him with his paintings. I had already such a liking for this art that our schoolmates called José Guevarra, another pupil, and myself the class painters.

CHAPTER III

My Daily Life in Biñan

Many of us lived in the same house. There were my aunt, two cousins, and three half-cousins. My aunt was a very old lady, over seventy. She used to sit on the floor and read the Bible in Tagalog. One cousin was a maiden lady who liked very much to go to confession and to do penances. The other cousin, her brother, was a widower.

Rizal Monument, Biñan. It stands in front of Rizal's maternal grandfather's house

One of the half-cousins was something of a tomboy. She was quick to anger but frank and true-hearted. At times, we young folks played in the street at night. Our elders did not permit us to play in the house. The tomboy was two or three years older than I and taught me games. She always treated me as if I were her brother.

Santa Rosa Gate, on the road from Kalamba to Biñan.

My manner of life was simple. I heard mass at four if there were a service so early, or studied my lessons at that hour and went to mass afterwards. Then I went out in the yard and looked for mabolos. Then came breakfast, which generally consisted of a plate of rice and two dried sardines. There was class work till ten o'clock and after lunch a study period. In the afternoon, there was school from two o'clock until five. Next, there would be play with my cousins for a while. Study and perhaps painting took up the remainder of the afternoon. By and by came supper, one or two plates of rice with a fish called ayungin. In the evening we had prayers and then, if it was moonlight, a cousin and I would play in the street with the others. Fortunately, I was never ill while away from home. From time to time, I went to my own village. How long the trip seemed going, and how short coming back!

Many things happened which it would be tiresome to read. Finally, there came a letter from my sister Saturnina which announced that the steamer Talim would stop for me on a certain day. I said good-bye to my numerous friends and teacher. To my teacher, I expressed my sadness in leaving and my gratitude for his instruction. Although he had punished me frequently, he did so, I now think, out of the kindness of his heart; and his heart was heavy when he did it.

Statuette modeled in Dapitan from a street scene.

I left Biñan on Saturday afternoon, the seventeenth of December, 1870. I was then nine years old. For the first time, I saw what a steamer really was. It seemed to me most beautiful and in every way admirable. But I heard my cousin, who was with me, make remarks to the *banquero* that were not complimentary to her speed. I was the only passenger from Biñan. Two sailors put my baggage into a cabin. Then I went to inspect it. I thought I was going to be without a cabin-mate, but a Frenchman, Arturo Camps, who was a friend of my father, looked after me. The journey seemed very long, but finally we arrived at Kalamba.

Oh! how glad I was to see the shore! At once I wanted to jump into the first banca. A deckhand took me in his arms and put me into the captain's boat. Then the Frenchman came and four sailors rowed us ashore. It is impossible to describe my joy when I saw a servant waiting for us with a carriage. I jumped in and soon found myself again in our home, happy in the love of my family. Here end my recollections of that period of mingled sadness and gladness, in which, for the first time, I came to know anybody of foreign birth.

CHAPTER IV

THE INJUSTICE DONE MY MOTHER

(This chapter and the next one, Rizal wrote in 1879. At that time he was eighteen years old.)

Some days after my return to Kalamba, my parents decided that I should remain, and that later, I should go to Manila. I wanted to study with a teacher of the town, even though I could learn no more than multiplication, so I entered the village school.

Rizal's uncle. He was educated at a Calcutta English school. He was a friend of the liberal Spanish leaders of his time.

Rizal's uncle inherited this home in Biñan from Rizal's grandfather. Once the largest dwelling in Biñan, it is now a cinematograph and the home of two families. The Rizal monument stands in front of it.

Guardia Civil soldier.

At this time, an uncle of mine, Don José Alberto, returned from Europe. He found that during his absence, his wife had left his home and abandoned her children. The poor man anxiously sought his wife and, at my mother's earnest request, he took her back. They went to live in Biñan. Only a few days later the ungrateful woman plotted with a Guardia Civil officer who was a friend of ours. She accused her husband of poisoning her and charged that my mother was an accomplice. On this charge, the alcalde sent my mother to prison.

I do not like to tell of the deep grief which we all, nine sisters and brothers, felt. Our mother's arrest, we knew, was unjust. The men who arrested her pretended to be friends and had often been our guests. Ever since then, child though I was, I have distrusted friendship. We learned later that our mother, away from us all and along in years, was ill. From the first, the alcalde believed the accusation. He was unfair in every way and treated my mother rudely, even brutally. Finally, he persuaded her to confess to what they wished by promising to set her free and to let her see her children. What mother could resist that? What mother would not sacrifice life itself for her children?

They terrified and deceived my mother as they would have any other mother. They threatened to condemn her if she did not say what they wished. She submitted to the will of her enemies and lost her spirit. The case became involved until the same alcalde asked pardon for her. But this was only when the matter was before the Supreme Court. He asked for the pardon because he was sorry for what he had done. Such was his meanness that I felt afraid of him. Attorneys Francisco de Marcaida and Manuel Masigan, Manila's leading lawyers, defended my mother and they finally succeeded in having her acquitted. They proved her innocence to her judges, her accusers and her hosts of enemies. But after how much delay?— After two and a half years.

Rizal's Mother.

Meanwhile my father decided to send me to Manila with my brother Paciano. I was to take the entrance examinations for the secondary course in the Ateneo Municipal. I arrived in Manila on June 10th, 1872. I found out for the first time what examinations were like. My examinations were in Christian doctrine, arithmetic and reading, in San Juan de Letran College. They gave me a passing mark and I returned to my home. A few days later came the celebration of the town festival, after which I went to Manila. But even then, I felt that unhappiness was in store for me.

Rizal's Father

Rizal's signature, from a letter written in London
when 28 years of age.

CHAPTER V

A STUDENT IN MANILA

As I had hoped, I was taken to the Jesuit priest at that time in charge of the Ateneo Municipal. He was Father Magin Fernando. At first he was unwilling to admit me. One reason was I had come late. Other reasons were that I did not seem strong and was very small for my age. I was then eleven. But later, Doctor Manuel Xeres Burgos, a nephew of the ill-fated Padre Burgos, spoke in my favor; and Father Fernando admitted me.

I dressed myself in the uniform like the other students, wearing a white coat, or americana, and a necktie, and entered the chapel of the Jesuit Fathers to hear mass. What fervent prayers did I address to God!

An Ateneo Professor modeled by Rizal in Dapitan from memory. This bust won a gold medal at the St. Louis Exposition, in 1904

After mass, I went to the classroom. There I saw a number of boys, Spanish, mestizos and natives, and a Jesuit teacher. Father José Bech, the teacher, was a tall man, thin and somewhat stooping, but quick in his movements. His face was thin and pale, yet lively. His eyes were small and sunken, his nose sharp and Grecian. His thin lips curved downwards. He was a little eccentric, sometimes being out of humor and intolerant; at other times amusing himself by playing like a child.

Some of my schoolmates were interesting enough to warrant mentioning them by name. Florencio Gavino Oliva, a young man from my own province, had great talent but he did not work steadily. The same thing was true of Moisés Santiago, a mathematician and a penman. It was also true of Gonzalo Manzano, who then held the position of "Roman Emperor."

Rizal's favorite teacher in the Ateneo. Father Sanchez visited Rizal in his exile in Dapitan, and helped him start a school for the Dapitan boys

In Jesuit colleges they divide the boys into two groups or "empires,"— one Roman and the other Greek. These two "empires" are always at war. The boys of one "empire" always want to outdo those of the other empire in all kinds of contests. Each group has a leader who is called "Emperor." The "Emperor" wins his place by doing the best work and standing the highest of anyone in his group. I was put at the end of the line. I could scarcely speak Spanish, but I already understood it.

After the religious exercises, I went out and found my brother waiting to take me to my lodgings, which were about twenty-five minutes' walk from the college. My brother did not wish to leave me in the Walled City, which seemed very gloomy to me.

I lodged in a small house on Calle Caraballo, near an estero. The house consisted of a dining room, a sala, a bedroom and a kitchen. An awning covered the small space between the door and the steps. My landlady was a maiden lady called Titay, who owed our family three hundred pesos. Her mother, a good old woman, lived with her. There were besides a crazy woman, quite harmless, and some Spanish mestizos in the house.

I must not speak of my sufferings, or of my troubles and pleasures. I shall record only what happened in school during that year. By the end of the first week, I was going up in the class. Then I began to spend the siesta-time studying at Santa Isabel College. For this, I paid three pesos a month. I went there with Pastor Millena, a boy of my own age. A month later, I was "Emperor".

How pleased I was when I won my first prize, a religious picture! In the first quarter I gained another prize, with the grade "Excellent." After that I did not care to apply myself. I had foolishly become dissatisfied because of something my teacher said. Unfortunately, this continued until the end of the year and I gained only second place in all my subjects. This gave me the grade of "Excellent" but without any prize.

I spent the vacation at home and went with my eldest sister, Nening, to Tanawan, for the town festival. This was in 1873. But our pleasure was marred by the fact that our mother was not with us. I had gone alone to see my mother without first sending word either to her or to my father. This was at the close of the term in which I held second place. I thought with what joy I would surprise her. Instead, we wept in each other's arms. We had not seen each other for more than a year.

After vacation was over, I returned to Manila and enrolled in the second year. Then I hunted lodgings in the Walled City. It was too tiring to live so far away. I found a place at 6 Calle Magallanes in the house of an elderly widow, Doña Pepay. Her daughter, also a widow, lived with her. The name of the daughter was Doña Encarnación, and her four sons were José, Rafael, Ignacio, and Ramón.

Nothing worth telling happened that year. My professor was the same as in the previous year; but I had different schoolmates. Among them I found three who had been with me in Biñan. At the end of this year, I won a medal and returned to my town.

I again went alone to visit my mother in prison. Like another Joseph, I prophesied to her from a dream that her release would take place within three months. This prediction happened to come true.

At this time, I began to devote my leisure to reading novels. Years before, I had read one, but it was not with any great interest. Imagine how a romantic youngster of twelve would delight in the Count of Monte Cristo! Under the pretext that I should have to study general history, I persuaded my father to buy me a set of Cesar Cantu y Diós' histories.

I gained much by reading them. In spite of my only half applying myself and of my indifferent Spanish, I was able to win prizes in the quarterly examinations. I should have gained the medal if I had not made some slips in Spanish, which I spoke very poorly. This gave the place to a Spanish lad who spoke his mother tongue better than I could. Thus, then, I finished my third year.

When I next returned to Manila, I found my former landlady's house full. I had to take a room in the house with my brother, Paciano Mercado, in company with a boy from my town named Quintero. My life was not so free as formerly, for I was under close supervision. The regular hours, however, were better for me. I prayed and played with my landlord's children.

A portrait of General Paciano Rizal-Mercado should appear here, but he has never had his picture taken. In September, 1896, he was cruelly tortured in an unsuccessful endeavor to get him to sign a statement that his brother was the leader of the rebellion. Rizal's last letter, from the Fort Santiago death-cell, tells how much the younger brother owed to the elder:

"My dear brother: Now that I am about to die, it is to you that I write my last letter. I am thinking of how you worked to give me my career....

... I believe that I have tried not to lose my time ... I know how much you have suffered for my sake. ... I assure you, brother, that I die innocent of this crime of rebellion."

Carving of the Sacred Heart of Jesus, made by Rizal while in the Ateneo. Even then he was the hero of his schoolmates and the little image was long kept, as here shown, on the door of the students' dormitory. In 1896 his former teachers removed it and took it to him in the death cell at Fort Santiago

A little later my mother was proved innocent and she was set free. She came to embrace me as soon as she was free. After the vacation, in that memorable year of my mother's release, I again had my lodgings in the Walled City. The house was in Calle Solana and belonged to a priest. My mother had not wanted me to return to Manila, saying that I already had sufficient education. Did she have a presentiment of what was going to happen to me? Can it be that a mother's heart gives her double vision?

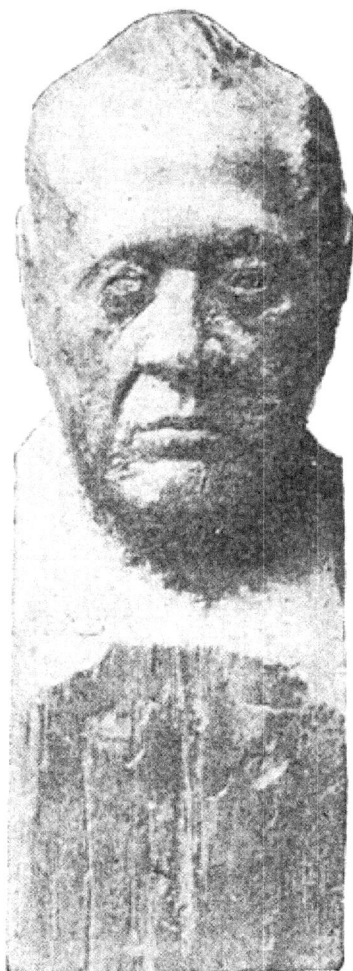

Bust of his father, made by Rizal when 14

My future profession was still unsettled. My father wanted me to study metaphysics, so I enrolled in that course. But my interest was so slight that I did not even buy a copy of the textbook. A former schoolmate, who had finished his course three months before, was my only intimate friend. He lived in the same street as I did. My companions in the house were from Batangas and had only recently arrived in Manila.

On Sundays and other holidays, this friend used to call for me and we would spend the day at my great-aunt's house in Trozo. My aunt knew his father. When my youngest sister entered La Concordia College, I used to visit her, too, on the holidays. Another friend had a sister in the same school, so we could go together. I made a pencil sketch of his sister from a photograph which she lent me. On December 8th, the festival of La Concordia, some other students and I went to the college. It was a fine day and the building was gay with decorations of banners, lanterns and flowers.

Rizal as a painter. This portrait is from a group picture of students who lived in the house of Rizal's cousin, Antonio Rivera. Rizal was then eighteen years old.

Shortly after that, I went home for the Christmas holidays. On the same steamer, was a Kalamba girl who had been a pupil in Santa Catalina College for nearly five years. Her father was with her. We were well acquainted but her schooling had made her bashful. She kept her back to me while we talked. To help her pass the time, I asked about her school and studies but I got hardly more than "yes" and "no" in answer. She seemed to have almost, if not entirely, forgotten her Tagalog. When I walked into our house in Kalamba, my mother at first did not recognize me. The sad cause was that she had almost lost her sight. My sisters greeted me joyfully and I could read their welcome in their smiling faces. But my father, who seemed to be the most pleased of all, said least.

The next day we were expecting friends from Manila to arrive, on their way to Lipa. But the steamer landed its passengers at Biñan because of a storm. So I saddled a pony and rode over there to meet them. My horse proved to be a good traveler and when I got back to Kalamba I rode on, by the Los Baños road, to our sugar mill. There I tied the horse by the roadside and for a time watched the water flowing through the irrigation ditch. Its swiftness reminded me of how rapidly my days were going by. I am now twenty years old and have the satisfaction of remembering that in the crises of my life I have not followed my own pleasure. I have always tried to live by my principles and to do the heavy duties which I have undertaken.

MY FIRST READING LESSON

This tells how he himself became an intelligent student. It was probably written while he was studying the schools of Saxony. These were the models for America so that the present educational system here is along the lines he advocated. As a child he had written a poem, "By Education the Fatherland Gains in Splendor".

I remember the time when I had not seen any other river than the one near my town. It was as clear as crystal, and joyous, too, as it ran on its course. But it was shaded by bamboos whose boughs bent to every breeze as if always complaining. That was my only world. It was bounded at the back by the blue mountains of my province. It was bounded in front by the white surface of the lake. The lake was as smooth as a mirror. Graceful sails were to be seen everywhere on it.

At that age, stories pleased me greatly and, with all my soul, I believed whatever was in the books. There were good reasons why I should. My parents told me to be very careful of my books. They urged me to read and understand them. But they punished me for the least lie.

My first recollection of reciting my letters reaches back to my babyhood. I must have been very little then, for when they rubbed the floor of our house with banana leaves I almost fell down. I slipped on the polished surface as beginners in skating do on ice. It took great effort for me to climb into a chair. I went downstairs step by step. I clung to each round of the baluster.

In our house, as in all others in the town, kerosene oil was unknown. I had never seen a lamp in our town, nor a carriage on our streets. Yet I thought Kalamba was a very gay and lively town. One night, all the family, except my mother and myself, went to bed early. Why, I do not know, but we two remained sitting alone. The candles had already been put out. They had been blown out in their globes by means of a curved tube of tin. That tube seemed to me the finest and most wonderful plaything in the world. The room was dimly lighted by a single light of coconut oil. In all Filipino homes such a light burns through the night. It goes out just at day-break to awaken people by its spluttering.

My mother was teaching me to read in a Spanish reader called "The Children's Friend." This was quite a rare book and an old copy. It had lost its cover and my sister had cleverly made a new one. She had fastened a sheet of thick blue paper over the back and then covered it with a piece of cloth.

This night my mother became impatient with hearing me read so poorly. I did not understand Spanish and so I could not read with expression. She took the book from me. First she scolded me for drawing funny pictures on its pages. Then she told me to listen and she began to read. When her sight was good, she read very well. She could recite well, and she understood verse-making, too. Many times during Christmas vacations, my mother corrected my poetical compositions, and she always made valuable criticisms.

I listened to her, full of childish enthusiasm. I marveled at the nice-sounding phrases which she read from those same pages. The phrases she read so easily stopped me at every breath. Perhaps I grew tired of listening to sounds that had no meaning for me. Perhaps I lacked self-control. Anyway, I paid little attention to the reading. I was watching the cheerful flame. About it, some little moths were circling in playful flights. By chance, too, I yawned. My mother soon noticed that I was not interested. She stopped reading. Then she said to me: "I am going to read you a very pretty story. Now pay attention."

On hearing the word "story" I at once opened my eyes wide. The word "story" promised something new and wonderful. I watched my mother while she turned the leaves of the book, as if she were looking for something. Then I settled down to listen. I was full of curiosity and wonder. I had never even dreamed that there were stories in the old book which I read without understanding. My mother began to read me the fable of the young moth and the old one. She translated it into Tagalog a little at a time.

My attention increased from the first sentence. I looked toward the light and fixed my gaze on the moths which were circling around it. The story could not have been better timed. My mother repeated the warning of the old moth. She dwelt upon it and directed it to me. I heard her, but it is a curious thing that the light seemed to me each time more beautiful, the flame more attractive. I really envied the fortune of the insects. They frolicked so joyously in its enchanting splendor that the ones which had fallen and been drowned in the oil did not cause me any dread.

My mother kept on reading and I listened breathlessly. The fate of the two insects interested me greatly. The flame rolled its golden tongue to one side and a moth which this movement had singed fell into the oil, fluttered for a time and then became quiet. That became for me a great event. A curious change came over me which I have always noticed in myself whenever anything has stirred my feelings. The flame and the moth seemed to go farther away and my mother's voice sounded strange and uncanny. I did not notice when she ended the fable. All my attention was fixed on the fate of the insect. I watched it with my whole soul. I gave to it my every thought. It had died a martyr to its illusions.

As she put me to bed, my mother said: "See that you do not behave like the young moth. Don't become disobedient, or you may get burnt as it did." I do not know whether I answered or not. I don't know whether I promised anything or whether I cried. But I do remember that it was a long time before I fell asleep. The story revealed to me things until then unknown. Moths no longer were, for me, insignificant insects. Moths talked; they knew how to warn. They advised, just like my mother. The light seemed to me more beautiful. It had grown more dazzling and more attractive. I knew why the moths circled the flame.

The advice and warnings sounded feebly in my ears. What I thought of most was the death of the heedless moth. But in the depth of my heart I did not blame it. My mother's care had not had quite the result she intended.

Years have passed since then. The child has become a man. He has crossed the most famous rivers of other countries. He has studied beside their broad streams. He has crossed seas and oceans. He has climbed mountains much higher than the Makiling of his native province, up to perpetual snow. He has received from experience bitter lessons, much more bitter than that sweet teaching which his mother gave him. Yet, in spite of all, the man still keeps the heart of a child. He still thinks that light is the most beautiful thing in creation, and that to sacrifice one's life for it is worth while.

Rizal's sacrifice of his life, on the Luneta, Manila, December 30th, 1896. He is now buried, in the imposing Rizal Mausoleum, near the scene of his execution.

Professor José Burgos. He was unjustly executed in 1872. Of him, Rizal wrote:
"He awakened my intellect and made me understand goodness and justice. His farewell words I shall always remember: 'I have tried to pass on to you what I received from my teachers. Do you now do the same for those who come after you?'"

MY CHILDHOOD IMPRESSIONS

One of numerous rough drafts evidently written for practice. Published as "Mi Primer Recuerdo," in El Renacimiento, Manila, February 2, 1908.

I spent many, many hours of my childhood down on the shore of the lake, Laguna de Bay. I was thinking of what was beyond. I was dreaming of what might be over on the other side of the waves. Almost every day, in our town, we saw the Guardia Civil lieutenant caning and injuring some unarmed and inoffensive villager. The villager's only fault was that while at a distance he had not taken off his hat and made his bow. The alcalde treated the poor villagers in the same way whenever he visited us.

We saw no restraint put upon brutality. Acts of violence and other excesses were committed daily. The officers whose duty it was to protect the people and keep the public peace were the real outlaws. Against such lawbreakers, our authorities were powerless. I asked myself if, in the lands which lay across the lake, the people lived in this same way. I wondered if there they tortured any countryman with hard and cruel whips merely on suspicion. Did they there respect the home? Or over yonder also, in order to live in peace, would one have to bribe tyrants?

The Lake, Laguna de Bay, from the Kalamba shore. Rizal's brother, General Paciano Rizal-Mercado, cleared this region of Spanish soldiers after Dewey's victory and then told the people to go to work. He set the example by again becoming a farmer.

THE SPANISH SCHOOLS OF MY BOYHOOD

From the introduction which Doctor Rizal put to his Spanish version of an article on "The Transliteration of Tagalog". His advocacy of the English style used in other Malay countries as more akin to the genius of Filipino dialects was considered extremely unpatriotic by most Spaniards.

Pencil Sketch of a Manila School Girl.

You perhaps attended a village Spanish school to learn your letters. Possibly, you have had to teach the letters in Spanish to others smaller than yourself. In either case, you must have noticed what I have, that children find great difficulty in mastering certain syllables. These are ca, ce, ci, co, ga, ge, gua, gui, etc. It is because Filipino children do not understand the reasons for such irregularities. Nor do they know the cause for the changes in value of the sounds of certain consonants.

Rizal when he was with Dr. Pardo de Tavera, in Paris, in 1889.

In the old times, blows fell like rain. Many pupils were whipped every day. Sometimes the schoolmaster broke the ferule and sometimes he broke the children's hands. The first pages of their primers fell to pieces from long and hard use. The children cried. Even the monitors had to suffer at times. Yet those syllables which cost the children so many tears are of no use to them.

Those syllables are necessary only in the learning of Spanish, which language in my time only three boys in a thousand ever really learned. These three learned it in Manila, by hearing Spanish spoken, and by committing to memory book after book. I often wondered what was the use of learning it at all when in the end one spoke only Tagalog. But I kept my wonder to myself. I felt that to try to make reforms in the Philippines at that time would be to embark on a stormy voyage.

After I grew up, I had to write letters in Tagalog. I was shocked at my ignorance of its spelling. I was surprised, too, to find the same word spelled differently in the different works which I consulted. This proved to me how foolish it was to try to write Tagalog in the Spanish way. The spelling in use today by all Filipino scholars is a great improvement over the old style. I want to place the credit for this change where it belongs. These improvements are due to the studies in Tagalog of Dr. T. H. Pardo de Tavera alone. I have only been one of the most zealous champions of the change from the Spanish style.

THE TURKEY THAT CAUSED THE KALAMBA LAND TROUBLE

This account was given Captain Carnicero, the Spanish commander of the Dapitan district where Rizal was in exile, in 1892.

My father was a friend of the owners of the Kalamba estate. He was intimate, too, with the manager in charge of the plantation. Frequently, important visitors came to the plantation house. Then the manager asked my father for whatever he needed. He very often asked for a turkey, and my father gladly gave it to him. The poultry yard at our house was always full of turkeys because my father was a fancier of these fowls.

Rizal at 30
Doctor Blumentritt considered this the best likeness among all the portraits of Rizal

But one season there came some epidemic and almost all the turkeys died. Only a few pairs, which were being kept for breeding, were left. Just at this time the manager one day sent for the customary turkey. Naturally my father had to tell the messenger that he had no turkeys to spare, because the greater part of them had died. This reply made the manager furiously angry. He wound up his abuse by saying, "You will pay for this in the end!" A few days later my father received a note from the manager, saying that he was going to raise the rent on the land which my father occupied. He said the rent would be one-third more than father was then paying.

The reason for this decision was clear. It was because my father had refused to give the manager the turkey. The proof of this was that no other tenant received any such notice.

Father paid this increase on the day set, without a single word of protest, being among the first to pay. But after a few months, there came another note. In it the manager gave notice that the rent would be doubled. This, he said, was because my father was growing rich from the rented land where he had installed machinery for making sugar.

My father could not pay this price. Then he was summoned to appear in court; and finally the alcalde ordered him to leave the land. So he lost his houses and machinery, all because of a turkey.

FROM JAPAN TO ENGLAND ACROSS AMERICA

From letters written en route to his friend Mariano Ponce and first published in Manuel Artigas' Biblioteca Nacional Filipina, Manila, June, 1910.

Crayon portrait of Rizal's cousin, Leonore Rivera, to whom he was engaged. The drawing was made in 1882, just before he sailed for

Spain. During his absence, his letters were kept from her and she was told that Rizal had forgotten her in the gay life of Europe. This was done because her mother's advisers thought Rizal's political ideas made him unsuitable for a husband. Leonore finally consented to the marriage urged upon her instead, and when too late, through Rizal's return in 1887, learned how she had been deceived. She died not long afterwards, of a broken heart, it was said.

On February 28th, 1888, I arrived in Yokohama. A few moments after reaching the hotel, I received the card of the official in charge at the Spanish legation. I had not even had a chance to brush up when he called. He was very pleasant and offered to assist me in my work. He even invited me to live at the legation, and I accepted. If, at the bottom, there was a desire to watch me, I was not afraid to let them know all about myself. I lived at the legation a little over a month, and traveled in some of the nearby provinces of Japan. At times, I was alone; at others, with the Spanish official himself, or with the interpreter. While there, I learned to speak Japanese, and made a slight study of the Japanese theatre. After many offers of employment, which I refused, I sailed at last for America, about April 13th.

On the steamer, I met a half-Filipino family, the wife being a mestiza, the daughter of an Englishman named Jackson. They had with them a servant from Pangasinan. The son asked me if I knew "Richal," the author of Noli Me Tangere. Smiling, I answered that I did; and, as he began to speak well of me, I had to make myself known and say that I was the author. The mother paid me compliments, too. I made the acquaintance of a Japanese who was going to Europe. He had been a prisoner for being a radical and editor of an independent newspaper. As the Japanese spoke only Japanese, I acted as interpreter for him until we arrived in London.

During this voyage I was not seasick.

I visited the larger cities of America, where I saw splendid buildings. The Americans have magnificent ideals. America is a homeland for the poor who are willing to work.

I traveled across America, and saw the majestic cascade of Niagara. I was in New York, the great city, but there everything is new. I went to see some relics of Washington, that great man whom I fear has not his equal in this century.

I embarked for Europe on the "City of Rome", said to be the second largest steamer in the world. On board, a newspaper was published up to the end of the voyage.

I made the acquaintance of many people. They wondered at my taking about with me a foreigner who could not make himself understood. The Europeans and Americans were astonished to see how I got along with him. I could speak to every one in his own language and understand what he said.

MY DEPORTATION TO DAPITAN

First published in the Biblioteca National Filipina, Manila. The account was secretly sent by Rizal to his friends very shortly after his arrival at his place of exile. The reference to the school is from a letter to Doctor Blumentritt.

I arrived in Manila the 26th of June, 1892. It was on a Sunday, at 12 o'clock, noon. A number of carbineers, including a major, met me. A captain and a sergeant of the Guardia Veterana were there in civilian clothes. I disembarked with my luggage, and they inspected it at the custom house.

From there, I went to the Oriente Hotel. I occupied Room No. 22, which overlooks the Binondo Church.

That afternoon, at four, I presented myself to His Excellency, Governor-General Despujol. He told me to return at seven in the evening and I did so. He granted my petition for the liberty of my father, but not for the liberty of my brother and sisters. He told me to return on Wednesday evening at half past seven.

From there, I went to see my sisters. First I saw my sister Narcisa, afterwards Neneng (Saturnina). On the following day, Monday, at six o'clock in the morning, I was at the railway station, bound for Bulacan and Pampanga. I visited Malolos, San Fernando, and Tarlac. On the return I stopped at Bacolor, reaching Manila on Tuesday at five o'clock in the afternoon.

Seven-thirty on Wednesday saw me with His Excellency. But not even then did I get him to revoke the deportation decrees. Still he gave me hope for my sisters. As it was the festival of Saints Peter and Paul, our interview ended at 9:15. I was to present myself on the following day, at the same hour.

That day, Thursday, we spoke on unimportant matters. I thanked him for having revoked the order to banish my sisters and told him that my father and brother would come by the first mail-steamer. He asked me if I wished to return to Hongkong and I answered, "Yes". He told me to come again on Wednesday.

Wednesday he asked me if I persisted in my intention of returning to Hongkong. I told him that I did. After some conversation he said that I had brought political circulars in my baggage. I replied that I had not. He asked me who was the owner of the roll of pillows and petates with my baggage. I said that they belonged to my sister. He told me that because of them he was going to send me to Fort Santiago.

Don Ramón Despujol, his nephew and aide, took me in one of the palace carriages. At Fort Santiago Don Enrique Villamor, the commander, received me. He assigned me to an ordinary room containing a bed, a dozen chairs, a table, a washstand, and a mirror. The room had three windows. One, without bars, looked out on a court; another had bars, and overlooked the wall and the beach; the third served also as a door and had a padlock. Two artillerymen were on guard as sentinels. They had orders to fire on anyone who tried to make signs from the beach. I could not talk with anyone except the officer of the guard, and I was not allowed to write.

Don Enrique Villamor, the commander of the fort, gave me books from the library.

Each day the corporal of the guard proved to be a sergeant. They cleaned the room every morning. For breakfast, I had coffee with milk, a roll, and coffee-cake. Lunch was at 12:30, and consisted of four courses. Dinner was at 8:30, and was similar to the lunch. Commander Villamor's orderly waited on me.

On Thursday, the 14th, about 5:30 or 6 p. m., the nephew notified me that at ten o'clock that night I should sail for Dapitan. I prepared my baggage, and at 10 was ready, but as no one came to get me, I went to sleep. At 12:15, the aide arrived with the same carriage which had brought me there. By way of the Santa Lucia gate, they took me to the Malecon, where were General Ahumada and some other people. Another aide and two of the Guardia Veterana were waiting for me in a boat.

The "Cebu" sailed in the morning at nine. They gave me a good stateroom on the upper deck. Above the doors could be read "Chief". Next to my cabin was that of Capt. Delgras, who had charge of the party.

Ten from each branch of the military service were in the party. There were artillery, infantry of the 70th, 71st, 72nd, 73rd, and 74th regiments, carbineers, cavalry and engineers, and Guardia Civil. Of artillerymen there were at least twelve.

We were carrying prisoners loaded with chains, among whom were a sergeant and a corporal, both Europeans. The sergeant was to be shot because he had ordered his superior officer, who had misbehaved while in Mindanao, to be tied up. The soldiers who obeyed orders and tied the officer up were given twenty years' imprisonment; and the officer himself was dismissed from the service because he had let them tie him up.

I ate in my stateroom, the food being the same as the officers had. I always had a sentinel and a corporal on guard. Every night, Captain Delgras took me for a promenade on deck till 9 o'clock.

We passed along the east coast of Mindoro and the west coast of Panay. We came to Dapitan on Sunday, at seven in the evening. Captain Delgras and three artillerymen accompanied me in a boat rowed by eight sailors. There was a heavy sea.

The beach seemed very gloomy. We were in the dark, except for our lantern, which showed a roadway grown up with weeds.

In the town we met the governor, or commandant, Captain Ricardo Carnicero. There was also a Spanish ex-exile, and the practicante, Don Cosme. We went to the town hall, which was a large building.

My life now is quiet, peaceful, retired and without glory, but I think it is useful too. I teach reading, Spanish, English, mathematics and geometry to the poor but intelligent boys here. Moreover I teach them to behave like men. I have taught the men how to get a better way of earning their living and they think I am right. We have begun and success is crowning our trials.

The Plaza of Dapitan, Island of Mindanao. The townhall appears in the lower righthand corner. Rizal made a raised map of Mindanao Island on the plaza, to teach their home geography to the Dapitan people. The map has been restored by the Insular Government and a bronze tablet tells its history

ADVICE TO A NEPHEW

Written from Dapitan. Rizal took great interest in the education of his sisters' children and in Germany had made for them a translation into Tagalog of Hans Christian Andersen's fairy tales. This he embellished with many appropriate drawings and wrote out very plainly, making a book of eighty pages.

I think that I ought to mention to you a slight error which I have noticed in your letter. It is a little error which many in society make.

One should not say, "I and my sisters greet you," but "My sisters and I greet you." Always you have to put yourself last. You should say: "Emilio and I," "You and I," "My friend and I," and so on. For the rest, your letter is well written. In it you express your thoughts clearly. You use only the necessary words, and your spelling is good.

Keep on advancing. Learn, learn and think much about what you learn. Life is a very serious matter. It goes well only for those who have intelligence and heart. To live is to be among men, and to be among men is to strive.

But this strife is not a brute-like, selfish struggle,— nor with men alone. It is a strife with men, and at the same time with one's own passions. It is a struggle with the proprieties, with errors, with prejudices. It is a never-ending striving, with a smile on the lips and the tears in the heart.

On this battlefield, man has no better weapon than his intelligence. He possesses no more force than he has spirit. Bring out your intelligence, then, and improve it. Strengthen and educate yourself that you may be prepared for the struggle.

FILIPINO PROVERBS

The Proverbs and the Puzzles were published, with comments here omitted, in Truebner's Oriental Magazine, London, June and July issues of 1889.

Rizal's own English.

1. Low words are stronger than loud words.

2. A petted child is generally naked (i. e. poor).

3. Parents' punishment makes one fat.

4. New king, new fashion.

5. Man promises while in need.

6. He who believes in tales has no mind of his own.

7. The most difficult to rouse from sleep is the man who pretends to be asleep.

8. Too many words, too little work.

9. The sleeping shrimp is carried away by the current.

10. The fish is caught through the mouth.

FILIPINO PUZZLES

He carries me, I carry him.— The shoes.

A deep well filled with steel blades.— The mouth.

Mrs. José Rizal. Wood medallion by Rizal of his wife, made at Dapitan. Her maiden name was Josephine Bracken. She was Irish, but had been adopted by an American. Her foster father became blind and, in hope of recovering his sight, went to Dapitan. There Rizal became engaged to Josephine but could not marry her because a political retraction was required of him before the ceremony would be performed. They were finally married in Fort Santiago, half an hour before his execution. Mrs. Rizal gave Speaker Osmeña his first lessons in English. She died five years after her husband

RIZAL'S DON'TS

Condensed from the regulations of the Philippine League (Liga Filipino), a co-operative economic society which Rizal organized in Manila just before his deportation, in 1892.

DON'T gamble.
DON'T be a drunkard.
DON'T break the laws.
DON'T be cruel in any way.
DON'T be a rabid partisan.
DON'T be merely a faultfinding critic.
DON'T put yourself in the way of humiliation.
DON'T treat anyone with haughtiness or contempt.
DON'T condemn anyone without first hearing his side.
DON'T abandon the poor man who has right on his side.
DON'T forget those who, worthily, have come to want.
DON'T fail those without means who show application and ability.
DON'T associate with immoral persons or with persons of bad habits.
DON'T overlook the value to our country of new machinery and industries.
DON'T ever cease working for the prosperity and welfare of our native land.

A pipe which Rizal made, of chalk, in Fort Santiago for his last Christmas gift to his father

HYMN TO LABOR

(Written expressly for the exercises celebrating the erection of the pueblo of Lipa, Batangas, into a villa, but received too late to be used on that occasion.)— Translation by Charles Derbyshire.

Men:

    Now the east with light is reddening,
And to our fields and tasks we fare;
By the toil of man sustaining
Life and home and country there.
    Though the earth be hard and stubborn,
And the sun unpitying glow,
For our country and our homes
Love an easy way will show.

Chorus:

For his country in peace,
    For his country in war,
Let the Filipino work,
    Let him live, let him die.

Matrons:

    Go then joyous to your labor,
While the wife awaits you here;
With the children learning from her
To hold truth and country dear.
    When night brings you weary homeward
May peace and joy await you there;
But if fate unkindly frown,
She your stubborn task will share.

Chorus:

For his country in peace,
    For his country in war,
Let the Filipino work,

Let him live, let him die.

Maidens:
    Hail to labor! Blessed be it,
For it brings our country wealth;
May we ever hold it sacred,—
'Tis our country's life and health!
    If the youth would win our favor
By his work his faith be shown;
Only he who toils and struggles
Will support and keep his own.

Chorus:
For his country in peace,
    For his country in war,
Let the Filipino work,
    Let him live, let him die.

Boys:
    Show us then the way to labor,—
The road you ope to guide our feet;
So that when our country calls us,
We your task may then complete,
    And the old men then will bless us,
Saying: "They are worthy of their sires;
For the dead are honored most
By sons whom true worth inspires."

Chorus:
For his country in peace,
    For his country in war,
Let the Filipino work,
    Let him live, let him die.

Rizal at 27. From a Hongkong photo. Taken just after Governor-General Terrero, who admired the author of Noli Me Tangere, had advised Rizal to leave the Islands to escape enemies so powerful that even his protection might not insure safety. Rizal had dared to help the Kalamba tenants to answer fully and truthfully inquiries which the Government had made regarding their landlords

MEMORY GEMS FROM RIZAL'S WRITINGS

Without liberty there is no light.

One evil does not correct another.

My dearest wish is the happiness of my country.

It is a useless life which is not consecrated to a great idea.

A man keeps his independence while he holds to his own way of thinking.

If our country is ever to be free it will not be through vice and crime.

Knowledge is the heritage of mankind, but only the courageous inherit it.

It is better to honor a good man in life than to worship him after he is dead.

Resignation is not always a virtue; it is a crime when it encourages tyrants.

In the flames of war those who suffer most are the defenceless and the innocent.

I have worked for the good of my native land, I have consecrated my life to the welfare of others.

We need criticism to keep us awake. It makes us see our weaknesses so that we may correct them.

There are three ways in which one may accompany the course of progress: in front of, beside, or behind it.

Where are the young men who will consecrate their best years, their ambitions and their enthusiasms to the welfare of their native land?

Manila skyline. Rizal's last view of the city as the steamer, in 1882, was taking him to Spain. Drawn on shipboard

MARIANG MAKILING

(This story is a favorite in my town.)

Mariang Makiling was a young woman. She lived somewhere on the beautiful mountain Makiling, between Laguna province and Tayabas province. No one knew just where or how she lived. Some said she lived in a beautiful palace surrounded by gardens. Others said she lived in a poor hut made of nipa and bamboo.

Maria was tall and graceful. Her color was a clear, pure brown, kayumanging kaligatan, as the Tagalogs say. Her eyes were big and black. Her hair was long and thick. Her hands and feet were small and delicate. She was a fairy-like creature born under the moon-beams of the Philippines. She flitted in and out among the woods of Makiling. She was the ruling spirit of the mountain; but she seldom came within sight of man.

Hunters sometimes saw Maria on the night of Good Friday when they went out to trap deer. She would be standing motionless on the edge of some great cliff. Her long hair floated in the wind. She sometimes approached them. She would salute them gravely, then pass on and disappear among the shadows of the trees. They never dared to question her, to follow her, or to watch her.

She liked best to appear after a storm. Then she would scurry over the fields bringing back life to the fallen plants, and setting everything to rights. The trees straightened up their wind-blown trunks. The streams went back into their beds. All signs of the storm disappeared as she passed.

Mariang Makiling had a very good heart. She used to lend the poor country folk clothing or jewels for weddings, baptisms and feast days. All she asked in return was a pullet as white as milk. It had to be a dumalaga; that is, one that had never laid an egg.

Sometimes she appeared as a simple country girl and helped the poor old women to pick up firewood. Then she would slip gold nuggets, coins and jewels into their bundles of wood.

A hunter was one day chasing a wild boar through the tall grass and thorny bushes. Suddenly he came to a hut in which the animal hid. A beautiful young woman came out and said:

"The wild boar belongs to me. You have done wrong to chase it, but I see that you are very tired. Your arms and legs are covered with blood. Come in and eat. Then you may go on your way."

The man was charmed by the beauty of the young woman. He went in and ate everything she offered him. But he was not able to speak a single word. Before the hunter left, the young woman gave him some pieces of ginger. She told him to give them to his wife for her cooking. The hunter thanked her and put the roots inside the crown of his broad hat. On the way home his hat felt heavy. So he took out a number of the pieces and threw them away. He was surprised and sorry the next day when his wife discovered that what they had taken to be ginger was solid gold. The supposed roots were bright as rays of sunshine.

But Mariang Makiling was not always kind and generous to the hunters. Sometimes she punished them.

One afternoon two hunters were coming down the mountain, carrying some wild boars and deer which they had killed during the day.

They met an old woman who begged them to give her a quarter. They thought that was too much to give, so they refused. The old woman said that she would go and tell the mistress of those animals, and she left them. This threat made the hunters laugh heartily. When night had fallen and the two were near the plain, they heard a distant shout— very distant, as though it came from the top of the mountain:

"There they go-o-o— o!"

Then another even more distant cry replied:

"There they go-o-o— o!"

That cry surprised both the hunters, who could not account for it. On hearing it, the dogs stuck up their ears. They uttered low growls and drew nearer to their masters. In a few minutes the same cry was heard again, this time from the mountain-side. On hearing it, the dogs thrust their tails between their legs and came close to their masters. The men stared at each other without saying a word. They were astonished that the one who uttered the cry could travel so far in such a short time. When they reached the plain, the fearful cry was heard again. This time, it was so clear and distinct that both looked back. In the moonlight, they could see two strange, gigantic shapes coming down the mountain at full speed. Both hunters ran as fast as they could with such heavy loads. Still the strange creatures came nearer.

The men, coming to a spring called bukal, threw down their burdens, and climbed a tree; and the dogs fled toward the town. The monsters came up, and in a few seconds devoured the wild boars and deer and went back toward the mountain. Only then, did the hunters recover. The more courageous took aim but his gun missed fire and the monsters escaped.

No one ever knew whether Mariang Makiling had parents, brothers and sisters, or other kin. Such persons spring up naturally, like the stones the Tagalogs call mutya. No one ever knew her real name. She was simply called Maria. No one ever saw her enter the town or take part in any religious ceremony. She remained ever the same. The five or six generations that knew her always saw her young, fresh, sprightly, and pure.

For many years now no one has seen her on Makiling. Her vapor figure no longer wanders through the deep valleys. It no longer hovers over the waterfall on the serene moonlight nights. The melancholy tone of her mysterious harp is no longer heard. Now lovers are married without getting from her either jewels or presents. Mariang Makiling has disappeared.

Some blame the people of a certain town who not only refused to give her the customary white pullet but even failed to return the jewels and clothing borrowed. Others say that Mariang Makiling is offended because some landlords are trying to take half of the mountain.

Inkstand and pen-tray made, and used, by Rizal in Dapitan. He used it, too, in writing his last poem "My Last Thought" in Fort Santiago.

A CHRONOLOGY OF THE LIFE OF JOSÉ RIZAL

1848, June 28.— Rizal's parents married in Kalamba, La Laguna: Francisco Rizal-Mercado y Alejandra (born in Biñan, April 18,1818) and Teodora Morales Alonso-Realonda y Quintos (born in Sta. Cruz, Manila, Nov. 14, 1827).

1861, June 19.— Rizal born, their seventh child.

June 22.— Christened as JOSÉ PROTASIO RIZAL-MERCADO Y ALONSO-REALONDA.

1870, Age 9.— In school at Biñan under Master Justiniano Aquin Cruz.

1871, Age 10.— In Kalamba public school under Master Lucas Padua.

1872, June 10. Age 11.— Examined in San Juan de Letran college, Manila, which, during the Spanish time, as part of Sto. Tomás University, controlled entrance to all higher institutions.

June 26.— Entered the Ateneo Municipal de Manila, then a public school, as a day scholar.

1875, June 14. Age 14.— Became a boarder in the Ateneo.

1876, March 23. Age 15.— Received the Bachelor of Arts (B.A.) degree, with highest honors, from Ateneo de Manila.

June.— Entered Sto. Tomás University in Philosophy course.

1877, June. Age 16.— Matriculated in medical course. Won Liceo Artístico-Literario prize, in poetical competition for "Indians and Mestizos", with poem "To Philippine Youth."

Nov. 29.— Awarded diploma of honorable mention and merit by Royal Economic Society of Friends of the Country, Amigos del País, for prize poem.

1880, April 23. Age 19.— Received Liceo Artístico-Literario diploma of honorable mention for allegory "The Council of the Gods," in competition open to "Spaniards, mestizos and Indians." Unjustly deprived of first prize.

Dec. 8.— Operetta "On the Banks of the Pasig" produced.

1881. Age 20.— Submitted winning wax model design for commemorative medal for Royal Economic Society of Friends of the Country centennial.

Wounded in the back for not saluting a Guardia Civil lieutenant whom he had not seen. His complaint was ignored by the authorities.

Rizal at 22. From the first photo taken after his arrival in Spain.

1882, May 3. Age 21.— Secretly left Manila, with passport of a cousin, taking at Singapore a French mail steamer for Marseilles and entering Spain at Port Bou by railroad. Money furnished. by his brother, Paciano Mercado.

June.— Absence noted at Sto. Tomás University, which owned Kalamba estate. Rizal's father was compelled to prove that he had had no knowledge of his son's plan in order to hold the land on which he was the University's tenant.

July-Nov.— A student in Barcelona.

Nov. 3.— Began studies in Madrid.

1885, June 19. Age 24— Received degree of Licentiate in Medicine with honors from Central University of Madrid.

Rizal at 24. The original photograph was taken in Madrid.

1886, June. Age 25— Received degree of Licentiate in Philosophy, with honors and special mention in Latin, Greek, and Hebrew, from Central University of Madrid.

Clinical assistant to Dr. L. de Weckert, a Paris oculist.

Visited Universities of Heidelberg, Leipzig, and Berlin.

1887, Feb. 21. Age 26— Finished novel Noli Me Tangere in Berlin.

Travelled in Austria, Switzerland and Italy.

July 3.— Sailed from Marseilles.

Aug. 5.— Arrived in Manila. Travelled in nearby provinces with a Spanish lieutenant, detailed by the Governor-General, as escort.

1888, Feb.— Sailed for Japan via Hongkong.

Feb. 28.-Apr. 13. Age 27— A guest at Spanish Legation, Tokyo, and travelling in Japan.

Rizal at 26. From a photo taken in Switzerland.

April-May.— Travelling in the United States.

May 24.— In London, studying in the British Museum to edit Morga's 1609 Philippine History.

1889, March. Age 28.— In Paris, publishing Morga's History. Published "The Philippines A Century Hence" in La Solidaridad, a Filipino fortnightly review, first of Barcelona and later of Madrid.

1890, Feb.-July. Age 29.— In Belgium and Holland, finishing El Filibusterismo (The Reign of Greed), which is the sequel to Noli Me Tangere.

Published "The Indolence of the Filipino" in La Solidaridad.

Aug. 4.— Returned to Madrid to confer with countrymen on the Philippine situation, then constantly growing worse.

Rizal at 28. From a group picture, taken in Paris, with the Artist Luna's family.

1891, Jan. 27.— Left Madrid for France.

Nov. Age 30.— Arranging for a Filipino agricultural colony in British North Borneo.

Practiced medicine in Hongkong.

1892, June 26. Age 31— Returned to Manila under Governor-General Despujol's safe conduct.

Organized mutual aid economic society Liga Filipina.

July 6.— Ordered deported to Dapitan, but the decree and charges were kept secret from him.

Taught school and conducted a hospital during exile, patients coming from China coast ports for treatment. Fees thus earned were used to beautify the town. Arranged a water system and had the plaza lighted.

1896, Aug. 1. Age 35— Left Dapitan en route to Spain as a volunteer surgeon for the Cuban yellow fever hospitals. Carried letters of recommendation from Governor-General Blanco.

Aug. 7.–Sept. 3.— On Spanish cruiser Castilla in Manila Bay.

Sailed for Spain on Spanish mail steamer and just after leaving Port Said was confined to cabin as a prisoner on cabled order from Manila. (Governor-General Blanco's promotion had been purchased by Rizal's enemies to secure appointment of a governor-general subservient to them, the servile Polavieja.)

Oct. 5.— Placed in Montjuich Castle dungeon on arrival in Barcelona and the same day re-embarked for Manila. Friends and countrymen in London by cable made an unsuccessful effort for a Habeas Corpus writ at Singapore. On arrival in Manila was placed in Fort Santiago dungeon.

Dec. 3.— Charged with treason, sedition and forming illegal societies, the prosecution arguing that he was responsible for the deeds of those who read his writings.

Dec. 12.— Wrote poem "My Last Farewell" and concealed it in an alcohol cooking lamp, after appearing in a courtroom where the judges made no effort to check those who cried out for his death.

A Paris portrait of Rizal which appears on the 2-centavo stamped envelope. It is the only profile among his known portraits.

Dec. 15.— Wrote an address to insurgent Filipinos to lay down their arms because their insurrection was at that time hopeless. Address not made public but added to the charges against him.

Dec. 26.— Formally condemned to death by Spanish court martial.

Pi y Margall, who had been president of the Spanish Republic, pleaded with the Prime Minister for Rizal's life, but the Queen Regent could not forgive his having referred in one of his writings to the murder by, and suicide of, her relative, Crown Prince Rudolph of Austria.

Dec. 30.— Married in Fort Santiago death cell to Josephine Bracken, Irish, the adopted daughter of a blind American who came to Dapitan for treatment.

Age 35 years, 6 months, 11 days. Shot on the Luneta, Manila, at 7:30 a. m., and buried in a secret grave in Paco Cemetery. (Entry of death made on back flyleaf of Paco Church Register, among suicides.)

1897, Jan.— Commemorated by Spanish Freemasons who dedicated a tablet to his memory, in their Grand Lodge hall in Madrid, as a martyr to Liberty.

1898, Aug.— Grave sought, immediately after the American capture of Manila, by Filipinos who placed over it, in Paco cemetery, a cross inscribed simply "December 30, 1896." Since his death his name had never been spoken by his countrymen, but all references had been to "The Dead" (El Difunto).

Dec. 30.— Memorial services held by Filipinos, and American soldiers on duty carried their arms reversed.

1911, June 19.— Birth semi-centennial observed in all public schools by act of Philippine Legislature.

1912, Dec. 30.— Ashes transferred to the Rizal Mausoleum on the Luneta with impressive public ceremonies.

Rizal Mausoleum, Luneta, Manila. Here lies the body of José Rizal on the place of his execution, under a monument designed by the designer of the Swiss National Tell monument.

REFERENCES A READING LIST

RIZAL, JOSÉ.— *The Monkey and the Tortoise*. A Tagalog tale told in English and illustrated by Rizal. Manila, 1912.

— *Elias and Salome*. An unpublished chapter from the original Noli Me Tangere manuscript.

— *The Whole Truth*. (La Verdad para Todos.) A defense of the Filipinos.

— *By Telephone* (Por Teléfono). A satire.

— *The Philippines A Century Hence* (Filipinas Dentro de Cien Años). A forecast of the future.

— *The Indolence of the Filipino* (La Indolencia de los Filipinos). An answer to criticism.

— *My Last Thought and other Poems*. Translations by Charles Derbyshire and A. P. Fergusson.

— *Mariang Makiling*, A folk tale.

(These titles are in the *Noli Me Tangere Quarter-Centennial Series*, edited by Austin Craig. Translations are by Charles Derbyshire.) Manila, 1912.

— *An Eagle Flight: A Filipino Novel*. Adapted from Noli Me Tangere, with a short sketch of Rizal's life. Anonymous translator. New York, 1900.

Manuscript of Rizal's Great Novel, now in the Philippine Library.

El Filibusterismo is the second part, or sequel, of the novel Noli me tangere. Rizal's first novel told the Filipinos of their faults; this book warned Spain of the danger of losing her colony unless the colonial government became better. "Filibusterer" was the name given to Filipinos who wanted reforms in the government.

House where El Filibusterismo was begun. This sketch, made in pencil was enclosed in a letter from Los Baños to Prof. Blumentritt.

— Friars and Filipinos. An abridged translation of Noli Me Tangere by F.E. Gannett. New York, 1900.

— The Social Cancer. Charles Derbyshire's translation of Noli Me Tangere. Manila and New York, 1912.

— The Reign of Greed. Charles Derbyshire's translation of El Filibusterismo. Manila and New York, 1912.

BLUMENTRITT, F.— Life of José Rizal. Translated from the German by H.W. Bray. Singapore, 1898.

— Views of Doctor Rizal, the Filipino Scholar, upon Race Differences. Translated from the German by R.L. Packard. Popular Science Monthly, Vol. 61 (July, 1902), pages 222–229.

HALSTEAD, MURAT.— The Story of the Philippines. Pages 190–201 give a translation of Rizal's "The Vision of Friar Rodriguez" (La Visión de Fray Rodriguez) by F.M. de Rivas. Chicago, 1898.

CLIFFORD, SIR HUGH.— The Story of José Rizal, the Filipino. In Blackwood's Edinburgh Magazine, Vol. 172 (Nov., 1902), pages 620–638.

CRAIG, AUSTIN.— Readings from Rizal. A series of selections from Rizal's novels, in volume 1 of "The Philippine Teacher." Manila, 1905.

— The Rizal Story in Pictures. A series of twenty-one post cards with authentic illustrations and explanations. Manila, 1908.

— The Story of José Rizal, the Greatest Man of the Brown Race. Manila, 1909.

— Lineage, Life and Labors of José Rizal. Manila and Yonkers-on-Hudson, 1912.

— Particulars of the Philippines' Pre-Spanish Past. Dr. Rizal's "Ibn Batutu's Tawalisi the Northern Part of the Philippines" appears on pages 20–22. Manila, 1916.

CRAIG-FEE.— Rizal, the Martyr-Hero of the Philippines. An imaginative account, expanding the known facts, for youthful readers. In "Philippine Education." Manila, 1913.

BLAIR-ROBERTSON.— The Philippine Islands 1493–1898. Rizal's annotations to Morga's 1609 History of the Philippines appear among the notes in Vols. XV and XVI. Cleveland, Ohio, 1904.

Brief sketches of Rizal's life and work may be found in every encyclopedia published since 1898, the modern histories of the Philippines have extended references to him and the numerous recent works on the Philippines all attempt estimates of his influence upon his countrymen.

Diploma of Merit
won by
JOSÉ RIZAL

In a literary competition in honor of Spain's greatest writer, Cervantes, held in Manila in 1880, the Liceo Artistico-Literario offered a gold ring as first prize and the Economic Society of the Friends of the Country gave the winner a diploma of merit. Rizal's allegory, "The Council of the Gods" was preferred by the judges, all Spaniards. But when the envelopes containing the contestants' names were opened, there was objection to giving first prize to a Filipino when prominent Spaniards had taken part in the contest. Rizal says that he was hissed off the stage when he appeared in answer to the reading of his name. Manila newspapers of that period dared not speak of the incident openly but there were several veiled allusions to it. One writer sarcastically said that medical students should be forbidden to write poetry.

THE COUNCIL OF THE GODS

"We gods and goddesses, met on Mount Olympus, find that the greatest three authors in the world's history are of equal merit. So in justice equal respect must be paid them. To Homer we award fame's trumpet, to Vergil the lyre of glory, and to Cervantes the laurel wreath of immortal honor."

To the Philippine Youth

"Hold high the brow serene,
O youth, where now you stand;
Let the bright sheen,
Of your grace be seen,
Fair hope of my Fatherland!"

Prize, and the first verse of the winning poem, won by Rizal at the age of 17 in a public competition open to "Indians and Mestizos". By these two names, the Spaniard called, and divided, the Filipinos.

MY LAST THOUGHT

"Farewell, beloved Fatherland, thou sunny clime of ours,
Pearl of the Orient Ocean, our lost Paradise!
For thee my life I give, nor mourn its saddened hours;
And were't more bright, strewn less with thorns and more with flowers,
For thee I still would give it, a welcome sacrifice."

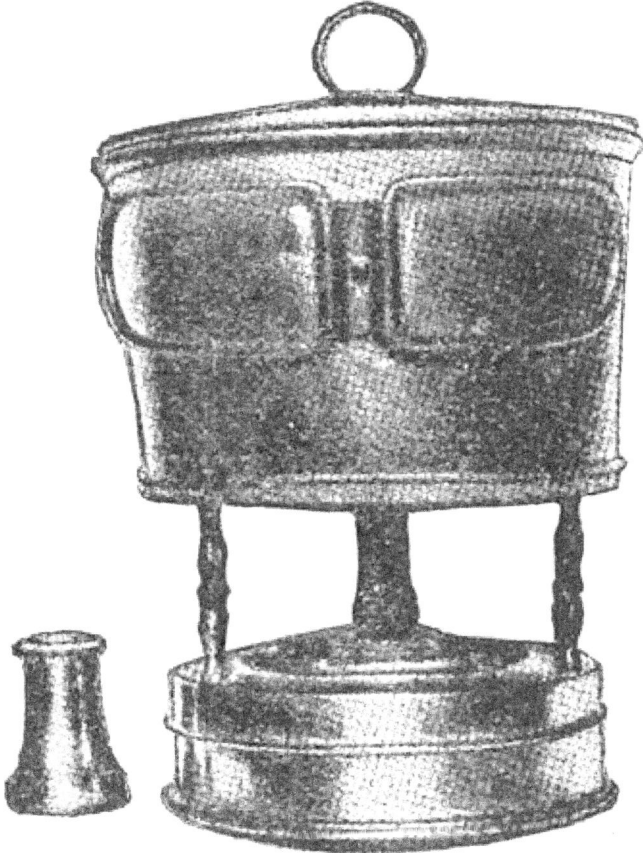

The alcohol lamp in which Rizal hid the poem, called "My Last Thought," which he wrote in the night after he learned that he was to die. The original poem, whose ink shows the effects of the alcohol, is now in the Philippine Library.

PHILIPPINE NATIONAL HYMN

Written in Spanish by José Palma

Music by I. Felipe

(The versifier of the English translation prefers not to have his name appear.)

Land that we hon - or, Born of the East - ern sun - rise,
Land of all bless - ings, Land of love and sun - shine,
Thy glo - rious ban - ner, Borne thru the fier - cest con - flicts,
Thy sun and stars shall Shine in thy sky for - ev - er,

Whose flam - ing spir - it Beats high with - in thy breast.
Thy sons and daugh - ters Safe in thy lap shall
Bright - ly il - lum - in'd, Guid - ed us from on high,
Lead - ing thy sons where Du - ty and hon - or

rest. And from thy vales and mount - ains green, And from thy seas and
lie. from thy vales and mount - ains green, And from thy seas and

skies,   the   song   of   thy   lov'd   lib - er - ty   for-
skies,   the   song   of   thy   lov'd   lib - er - ty   for-

ev - er   shall a-   rise.   And
ev - er   shall a-   rise.   E....... ...

qual - i - ty,   Fra - ter - ni - ty,   Free
rights of   Man   re - spect - ed   A ...

Press   and   Pub - lic   School   The......
land   the   Peo - ple   rule

HAIL, PHILIPPINES!

Words by L. H. Theobald

Music arranged from the Toreador's song in the opera "CARMEN"

Land of our Fath - ers, hail, all hail to thee! Palm shad - ed vale and bright spark - ling sea.
Land of the palm, thy fa - vor'd chil - dren see Glo - rious the dawn now ris - ing on thee.
Hail, star - ry em - blem, Ban - ner of the free! Thy folds pro - tect and bring lib - er - ty.

Thy sons on ev' - ry mount - ain side now sing, Hail, Phil - ip - pines! thy wood - lands
Sad tears our fath - ers shed are wiped a - way; Their groans and prayers bring us the
No more shall cruel op - pression's arm - ed hand Dark - en thy homes, dear native

ring! And let the ec - ho be "Thy loyal sons are we, U - nit - ed all and free"!
day Of peace and lib - er - ty, Joy and pros - per - i - ty, Thy sons shall all be free!
land, For wis - dom's path is free, And loyal sons are we, To live or die for thee!

HISTORICAL CONTEXT

INTRODUCTION TO THE 20TH CENTURY

The twentieth century brought significant upheaval in both society and literature. The two World Wars and the Great Depression, which devastated the entire world economy. The fall of the British Empire and the changes it brought to global politics, along with continued technical and scientific developments, all contributed to an unprecedented time of catastrophic transformation in human history.

Following World War I, a new disturbing and challenging type of poetry evolved, Imagism and Modernism emerged in the interwar era. Post-World War II saw the advent of numerous reactions to Modernism, notably the Postmodernism movement. Having left the Victorian era behind, the turn of the century witnessed the development of poets associated with the Georgian and Aesthetic movements.

LITERARY MOVEMENTS

THE EDWARDIAN ERA

The turn of the century, marked by Queen Victoria's death in 1901 and the accession of Edward VII, brought a sense of discontent and a shift away from the previous rigid Victorian convictions and conservatism. Albert Einstein, Charles Darwin, Sigmund Freud, Friedrich Nietzsche, and Karl Marx were among the time's most prominent philosophical, scientific, and political thinkers whose efforts had a significant and ground-breaking influence on Western culture, beliefs, and humanity's understanding of itself and its origins.

- H.G. Wells sparked modernism and a new era

As the 20th century and an unknown future arrived, people were both excited for the future and concerned about what transition may bring. In his early Utopian works, such as *Anticipations of the Reaction of*

Mechanical and Scientific Progress upon Human Life and Thought (1901), Mankind in the Making (1903), and Utopia (1905), English writer H.G. Wells examined and predicted the effects and transformations that science and technological advancement could bring.

- Realism and new topics in the arts

Pure Aestheticism was something that numerous writers during the Edwardian era, such as Dante Gabriel Rossetti, Oscar Wilde, and Algernon Charles Swinburne, consciously walked away from due to its slogan of "Art for Art's Sake," which was espoused by Decadent authors and artists near the end of the 19th century. Authors, particularly those of dramatic works, have recently begun to use their works as a platform for debate and study of the day's important moral and social issues, touching on a wide range of themes including politics, the role of women, marriage as a social institution, and the ethics of war.

Man and Superman (1903) and Major Barbara (1907) by George Bernard Shaw, Strife (1909) by John Galsworthy, and The Voysey Inheritance (1905) by Harley Granville Barker, were all heavily inspired by the realism and observational techniques of 19th century playwrights and writers such as Ibsen, Balzac, and Dickens.

- Traditionalism and transition

Like Rudyard Kipling and G.K. Chesterton, Thomas Hardy is an example of a writer who enjoyed literary acclaim in the 19th century. He could be thought of as a transitional character, bridging the divide between the Victorian and Edwardian eras by attempting to preserve conventional literary forms and techniques. A.E. Housman's pastoral poetry demonstrates comparable attempts to resurrect traditional techniques and subjects. In the early twentieth century, the Georgian poets, who included Rupert Brooke, Robert Graves, and Edmund Blunden, maintained a more traditional, moderate poetic style by continuing to use romantic and emotional methods.

- Literary works of Henry James and Joseph Conrad

Another major transitional character in literature who helped bridge the gap between realism and modernism is Henry James, a British novelist of American heritage whose writings are notable for focusing on the collision between the Old World and the New, and also between Americans and Europeans. His final three writings, The Wings of the Dove, The Ambassadors, and The Golden Bowl, published between 1902 and 1904, were filled with dread and despair about a new world order in which ancient social institutions and moral certitudes were vanishing. Joseph Conrad analyses the cost of human arrogance and failures in innovative works such as Heart of Darkness (1902), Nostromo (1907), and Under Western Eyes (1911), conveying a similar concern with the world.

MODERNISM IN LITERATURE

The early twentieth century was a time of literary experimentation and invention, as authors and poets sought to break free from the previous century's post-Romantic traditions and felt the impact of fresh philosophical, political, and scientific ideas.

- Imagism literary movement

The writing of the imagists, a collection of English and American poets united under the canopy of ideals advocated by Ezra Pound in his poetry anthologies Ripostes (1912) and Des Imagistes (1914), is an excellent illustration of this new modernist mindset. T. E. Hulme, Richard Adlington, Hilda Doolittle, and Amy Lowell were all important members. In their experimental poetry, they employed free verse and other unconventional forms.

- Modernist novels

The mood and subject matter of literary and lyrical works created after World War I started in 1914 to reflect the war's devastation. D.H.

Lawrence's modernist worldview may be observed in his extraordinary use of a stream-of-consciousness style, as shown in The Rainbow (1915) and Women in Love (1920), as well as his assessment of the disastrous ramifications of industrialisation. Ulysses, published in 1922 by James Joyce, also adopted the stream-of-consciousness style and successfully defined the modernist literary movement as a whole.

- Literature and World War I

Among the poets whose works were inspired by World War I were Rupert Brooke, whose patriotic poem 1914 effectively conveyed the idealistic nature of the war's initial months, Wilfred Owen, whose poems compellingly portray both the sense of camaraderie and the moral dilemmas of war, and Siegfried Sassoon, who captured the increasing feelings of rage and wastefulness as the war continued. Many of these works, however, were not well-known or recognized until the 1930s.

- T.S. Eliot's The Waste Land

T.S. Eliot is a modernist poet recognized for his use of innovative language and style. Through the use of a disconnected style and dissonant allusion to a diverse variety of literary and cultural works, Eliot brilliantly captured the discontentment and resentment observed from the viewpoint of the post-war era in two of his most renowned works, Prufrock and Other Observations (1917) and The Waste Land (1922). He acknowledged spiritual emptiness as the source of the psychological disease that is wreaking havoc on civilisation today, yet he nonetheless gave alternatives for rehabilitation and rebirth via the use of mythology and symbolism.

- 1920s and 1930s literature

The productions of modernist playwrights such as Eugene O'Neill, whose experimental techniques and use of naturalism and expressionist methods in his theatrical performances were extremely influential at the time, aided American theatre in reaching its zenith during the interwar period. Modernist poets of the time included E. E. Cummings and Wallace Stevens, while non-modernist authors included Theodore Dreiser, Ernest Hemingway, Scott Fitzgerald, and John Steinbeck. Hugh MacDiarmid, a Scottish poet, was a notable British author in the 1920s and 1930s, alongside Virginia Woolf, E. M. Forster, Evelyn Waugh, and P.G. Wodehouse.

Aldous Huxley's dystopian work Brave New World was released in 1932. Tropic of Cancer, Henry Miller's provocative book on his exploits as a struggling writer in Paris, was published two years later, in 1934. Graham Greene's Brighton Rock and James Joyce's Finnegans Wake were also released in 1938.

- Literature post World War II

Soon after World War II, a revitalized need for spiritual connection and religious conviction emerged as a basic and uniting literary theme, as indicated by works by such divergent novelists and poets including W.H. Auden, T.S. Eliot, Evelyn Waugh, and Christopher Fry.

- Novels in the 1940s and onwards

The first four volumes in Anthony Powell's 12-volume renowned cycle of novels A Dance to the Music of Time were released in the 1950s, while George Orwell's dystopian masterpiece on totalitarianism 1984 was first published in 1940. Lord of the Flies by William Golding (1954), The Prime of Miss Jean Brodie by Muriel Spark (1941), A Clockwork Orange by Anthony Burgess (1962), Watership Down by Richard Adams (1972), The Cement Garden by Ian McEwan, and Lanark by Alasdair Gray are other major works from the period between the middle of the 1950s and the late 1980s.

NOTABLE HISTORICAL EVENTS

- The assassination of Archduke Ferdinand

In 1914, the European superpowers were divided into the Triple Entente (France, Russia, and Britain) and the Triple Alliance (Germany, Austria-Hungary, and Italy). On June 28, a Bosnian Serb student assassinated Archduke Franz Ferdinand, the heir to the Austro-Hungarian throne, and his wife. This caused turmoil throughout the Balkan area. After Austria-Hungary declared war on Serbia on July 28, 1914, the Central Powers, the Ottoman Empire, Germany, and Austria-Hungary, and the Allies, Italy, Britain, France, Russia, and Serbia, were drawn into the battle.

- World War I

German plans for a quick victory over France were dashed when their forces were compelled to retreat when their advance was stopped outside of Paris. Following the huge German attack on Verdun in 1916 and the British campaign on the Somme the next year, which resulted in little advance and significant fatalities on both sides, both armies formed the Western Front, with trenches running from the English Channel to Switzerland.

The Eastern Front was raging in various locations, including the Italian Front, the Balkans Theatre, and the Middle Eastern Theatre. As a result of Germany's U-boats after the Allies' naval blockade, the United States joined the war in 1917, and Russia exited the war the following year after the October Revolution, allowing German forces to be sent to the Western Front.

Consequently, the German Army was unable to halt the Allies' assault. As a result, when Kaiser Wilhelm abdicated, the new German government accepted an Armistice in 1918, as did the other Central Powers.

The League of Nations was formed in 1919 to help avoid future conflicts, but Germany's catastrophic financial and territorial losses as a byproduct of the Treaty of Versailles fueled nationalist fervor and a desire to reclaim those lands. Economic and political instability may have also aided Adolf Hitler's ascent to power and expedited rearmament.

- World War II

Germany attacked Poland on September 1, 1939, led by German dictator Adolf Hitler. The United Kingdom and France joined the battle two days later, declaring war on Germany. As the German and British fleets continued their naval battle after rapidly seizing control of Poland, German U-boats targeted and sunk merchant ships destined for Britain.

In 1940, Germany successfully invaded Norway and advanced to France via Belgium and the Netherlands. Germany's army marched towards Paris, and Italy joined the fight against France and the United Kingdom. An armistice was signed a few days later.

In anticipation for the invasion, the German Luftwaffe aggressively bombarded Britain in what became known as the Blitz, but were eventually defeated by the Royal Air Force in the Battle of Britain, causing Hitler to postpone the assault.

While successfully seizing the Balkans and prepared to invade the Soviet Union, Hitler devised his "Final Solution" schemes for the genocide of Jews throughout Europe. During the next three years, over 4 million Jews perished in extermination camps in occupied Poland. A Soviet counterattack and adverse weather halted Hitler's Soviet advance in October 1941.

Japanese planes bombed Hawaii's Pearl Harbor naval base in December 1941, dragging the United States into war. Japanese victories following the US fleet's triumph at the Battle of Midway in June 1942, and subsequent US victories between 1942 and 1943, marked a turning point in the Pacific War.

By 1943, Allied troops had beaten the Italian and German forces in North Africa, and Mussolini's rule was destroyed in July 1943 with their invasion of Sicily and Italy. The Soviet counteroffensive on the Eastern Front effectively completed the Battle of Stalingrad in 1942, and the remaining German forces had surrendered by early 1943.

On D-Day, June 6, 1944, the Allies launched their invasion of Europe, landing tens of thousands of soldiers on the Normandy shores in France. After brutally bombing Germany from the air in February

1945, the Allies invaded the country on land, forcing Germany to formally surrender on May 8, 1945.

Fearing that a land invasion of Japan would result in even more catastrophic casualties, US President Truman authorized the deployment of the atomic bomb on Hiroshima and Nagasaki on August 15, 1945, resulting in the Japanese surrender on September 2.

- Women win right to vote in the UK

After a long battle led by campaigners such as suffragette Emmeline Pankhurst, an Act was passed in Parliament in 1918 allowing women in the United Kingdom the right to vote. The Representation of the People Act of 1918 made all men and women above the age of 30 eligible to vote. The Representation of the People (Equal Franchise) Act 1928, passed by the government in 1928, provides men and women over the age of 21 equal voting rights.

- The fall of the Berlin Wall

The Berlin Wall's fall on November 9, 1989, prompted both the melting of the Cold War and the breakdown of the Iron Curtain. Approximately three weeks later, at the Malta Summit, the Cold War was proclaimed formally finished. Furthermore, it heralds the end of communism in Central and Eastern Europe. On October 3, 1990, little over a year after the Berlin Wall fell, Germany's reunification was officially announced.

Made in the USA
Las Vegas, NV
31 January 2025